Pygmy Goats Made Easy:

Inclusive Guide on Pygmy Goats Fostering; Conduct, Health Issues, What They Eat, Lodging & Picking One as a Pet, Etc.

By

Mitchell T. Cudmore

Copyright@2021

TABLE OF CONTENTS

CHAPTER 1 4

   INTRODUCTION..4

CHAPTER 2 9

   DIETS AS WELL AS THE HOUSING/SHELTER REQUIREMENTS OF THE PYGMY GOATS........9

CHAPTER3 15

   THE BREEDING OF PYGMY GOATS 15

CHAPTER 4 20

   PROS AS WELL AS CONS OF YOUR AMAZING PYGMY GOATS & OTHER FACTS....................20

CHAPTER5 24

   THE PYGMY GOAT PRIZING & PROFIT, MILK AS WELL AS FOR MEAT 24

CHAPTER 6 29

THE PYGMY GOATS DISEASES OR AILMENTS
PLUS OTHER FACTS 29

CHAPTER 7 42

REARING CHICKENS WITH YOUR AMAZING
PYGMY GOATS 42

CHAPTER 8 76

CONCLUSION...76

THE END..77

CHAPTER 1

INTRODUCTION

Keen on raising Pygmy goats? In this total guide we walk you through all you require to know: where they come from, what they can be utilized for, where to get them, and considerably more!

The Pygmy goat is a little, solid, versatile goat breed that is progressively famous in the United States.

Their little size and benevolence make them appealing dairy goats, where they require less space and feed than bigger goats, and are reasonable for more modest homesteads in metropolitan and rural settings. They are additionally regularly kept as pets, basically for the satisfaction in their friendship.

The Origin of Pygmy Goats

The advanced Pygmy goat is regularly called the African Pygmy Goat, attributable to their beginnings in focal and West Africa. African raisers fostered these goats to be reduced and creative, and ready to get by on restricted great search in an assortment of environment conditions. Slid from West African and Nigerian Dwarf goats, pygmy goats were first brought into Europe through Britain, and ultimately to the United States.

They were initially imported as an oddity, for zoos and shows, and remain incredibly famous apparatuses in petting zoos the nation over because of their well disposed nature. Numerous Pygmy goats were embraced by private raisers during the

1950s, who checked out developing these adorable little goats as pets and friends.

They are too little to ever be a useful meat goat, and don't create as much milk as different varieties per lactation. Nonetheless, their milk has a high butterfat content, which makes them attractive dairy goats for cleansers, creams, and other goat milk items that require a high fat substance.

The Pygmy Goat Uses

The most mainstream use for pygmy goat is as pets and as partner creatures. They are adorable, versatile, cordial, and simple to really focus on.

Their little size makes them amazingly alluring 4H undertaking creatures, since kids are not threatened by these little goats.

They are additionally regularly kept as pleasant allies for touching creatures, where they give quieting kinship to other group creatures. Their flavourful milk makes them a welcome expansion in an assortment of little cultivating activities.

Pygmy goats are a most loved expansion to pastime homesteads and domesticated animals tasks, because of their little size, social nature, low-upkeep prerequisites and nice style.

Other Names: Miniature Goat, Nigerian Dwarf Goat

Size of Male: 60 lb - 86 lb; 19 to 24 inches

Size of Female: 53 lb - 75 lb; 18 to 22 inches

Ideal Habitat: Mildly muggy savannah zones with tall grasses

Fencing: Perimeter fence with intently divided wires

Incubation Period: 150 days

Raised for: Show creatures, vegetation control, pets, milk, meat, friend creatures (for different creatures)

With their restricted wellbeing concerns and pleasing nature, dwarf goats are among the most compensating animals to add to your pastime ranch or domesticated animals activity. They're an ideal "starter creature" for youths and simple to really focus on – ensure they have 1 to 2 lb of roughage daily and they'll flourish. Permit them to meander a field and play, and you're certain to get a lot of pleasure out of these great creatures.

CHAPTER 2

DIETS AS WELL AS THE HOUSING/SHELTER REQUIREMENTS OF THE PYGMY GOATS

Pygmy Goat Food Needs.

Water

Goats ought to consistently approach new, clean water. Recall that your pygmy goats will require more water than expected in sweltering climate or while lactating.

Search Plus feed

Pygmy goats will joyfully peruse on bushes, weeds, spices, and leaves. Permitting them opportunity of field likewise gives them the activity they need to remain solid and forestall medical issues.

Contingent upon the size of your field, the assortment of plants accessible, and the season, hay roughage can and ought to be offered with the expectation of complimentary taking care of. Buy exceptionally great roughage for the best goats and best quality milk.

Horse feed is high in calcium, which is fundamental when goats are joking and delivering milk. Horse feed can be costly, so a few groups supplement other great feed with hay pellets all things being equal.

Grain is an attractive wellspring of additional nourishment when a goat is creating milk, yet isn't rigorously fundamental.

Enhancements

Contingent upon the plants in your field, nearby soil piece, and dietary creation of your roughage, all things considered, your goats will require mineral enhancements. In the event that you are giving top notch food, they may just require limited quantities of minor elements.

At the point when free-took care of, goats will just eat as much mineral enhancements as they need. Utilize a mineral enhancement intended for goats or dairy cattle, and stay away from supplements intended for sheep, since goats and cows require copper, which is poisonous to sheep. You can likewise take care of your Pygmy goats products of the soil scraps from the kitchen to change up their eating regimen.

Pygmy goat nook needs

Like all goats, Pygmies are coordinated and prepared jumpers, and require plentiful space to meander and exercise to forestall pointless mileage on your fencing. Nonetheless, their little size restricts how high they can hop, and lessens the potential for harming your wall and nooks.

Recall that wall keep goats in, however should keep hunters out, and Pygmies are particularly defenceless to predation, contingent upon your neighbourhood natural life.

Indeed, even some lost canines can represent a danger to Pygmies. Wall ought to be around 4 feet high since Pygmy goats can't hop higher than that.

Goats will lean, stand, rub, and bite on fencing, especially in the event that they have more modest field, or if there is by all accounts alluring search on the opposite side, so posts ought to be no farther than 8 feet separated.

The most ideal approach to get your Pygmy goats is with a woven wire fence with 2x4-inch openings excessively little for grown-ups to put their heads through; woven wire is sufficiently able to withstand the biting, inclining, and standing that the fence will persevere. Woven/goat wire can be bought in rolls that are as of now 4 feet high.

Pygmy goat cover needs

All goats need cover around evening time and in helpless climate. Arrange your haven well away from your fence, so goats can't bounce from the top of their sanctuary over the fence, and try not to arrange the asylum on low ground that would amass downpour.

At least, the asylum can basically be a rooftop and three sides, with the goal that goats can escape terrible climate. It is smarter to have a dry soil floor than a wood one; wood ground surface can get elusive with mud or excrement, and possibly harm a goat or mess foot up.

They need extra asylum and assurance when they have joked, and to be independent from the group while the children are still little.

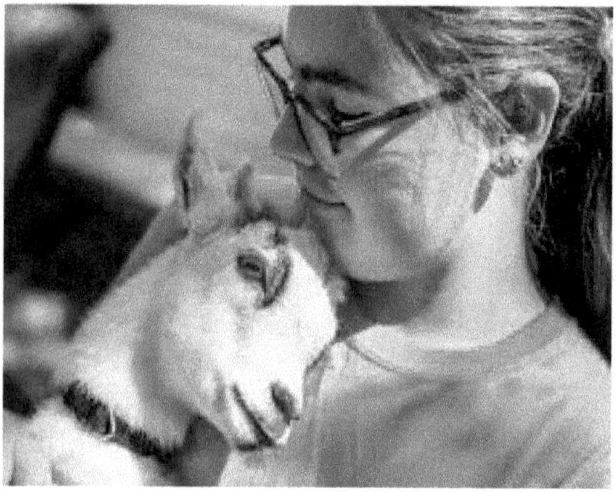

CHAPTER 3

THE BREEDING OF PYGMY GOATS

Pygmy goats' jars come into heat when they are just about as youthful as 2 months, however rearing them that early ought to be kept away from.

They are polyestrous, and will come into heat when they are presented to a male, so it's a smart thought to keep youthful does from bucks until you are prepared for them to raise.

They are productive reproducers, and jars bring forth 2-4 children each 9 a year.

At the point when a doe is coming into heat, she will by and large give indications with signature practices.

In the event that she is presented to a buck, she will for the most part show more prominent interest in him and search him out

Not at all like dairy goats that will come into heat yearly, and produce milk for 1-2 years, and Pygmy goats produced milk for just a generally short 3-multi month timeframe. This makes their polyestrous nature great.

In the event that you need a consistent stock of delightful, great goat milk, you will require a few does, and to time their reproducing plan so you will consistently have a doe delivering milk. At least, this implies four does, reproducing an alternate one each quarter, so you can have 1-2 quarts of goat milk a day consistently.

This presents the test that all goat ranchers have: keeping a buck so you can raise your goats when wanted, yet segregating him from the does so they don't raise to ahead of schedule, or more than once.

Indeed, even moderately little Pygmy bucks can be very decided when they need to get to an open doe, so their nook should be exceptionally strong. Furthermore, even bucks that should be isolated from the crowd actually have social requirements, and ought to be kept with different creatures or a wither for organization.

In the event that you decide to keep a buck, it is ideal to not have him share a fence with the does. Goats are ingenious, and have been known to raise through wall. Make a nook for the buck, with an unmistakable space of at least 15 feet among it and the fence in area for the does.

This support zone won't just forestall undesirable reproducing through the common fence, yet it will likewise deter him from assaulting the fence and putting unnecessary strain on it.

As another option, you may discover a neighbour with a buck and organize intermittent "dates" for your does when you are prepared for them to become game and to raise. This is a famous technique for keeping consistent milk creation, while staying away from a portion of the cost and challenge of possessing your own buck.

Pygmy does are popular for having joking issues, because of the little size of their pelvis, and should be observed intently as a pregnancy approaches its term. It is ideal to have a veterinarian accessible to help if important, and be acquainted with the indications of a troublesome joking and how best to mediate and help the doe.

Most does encountering a typical birthing will have a child inside an hour of starting work. In the event that your doe has been pushing for an hour and not yet joked, tell your veterinarian and have them on reserve. In the event that she actually has not conceived an offspring following 2 hours of pushing, it is important to mediate, and possibly save the existence of both mother and kid(s).

Pygmy goats make amazing and famous pets, and this prominence as a pet assists with lessening a portion of the pressure of sorting out how deal with the unnecessary male children conceived a few times each year. It is likewise a decent wellspring of extra pay from a pygmy goat's ranch.

CHAPTER 4

PROS AS WELL AS CONS OF YOUR AMAZING PYGMY GOATS & OTHER FACTS

Raising Pygmy goats: Pros and Cons

Like any creature, pygmy goats accompany a waitlist of advantages and disadvantages. Presently, contingent upon what you're utilizing the creature for, these rundowns could conceivably influence your choice to begin a homestead.

Pros for You

They're lively and dynamic animals. You'll never have a dull second with them.

Pygmy goats are clever and steadfast, which makes them ideal house pets.

They're one of only a handful few goat breeds that can repeat outside of their mating season.

Pygmy goats adjust effectively to their current circumstance.

The Cons

They require a ton of open space to go around and play.

Pygmy goats are viewed as prey among different creatures, so here and there they may experience difficulty coexisting with your different pets.

Pygmy goats care: Top instructions

Remember the accompanying tips when choosing if you need to add Pygmy goats to your life.

Since they're so small, dwarf goats don't require as much space as bigger varieties. Be that as it may, they do get exhausted effectively, so they'll require a space where they can go around and utilize their brains.

Pygmy goats ought to be kept in a ventilated, strong space worked for their size. They need a decent measure of freshwater every day to keep them sound. Additionally, a decent measure of hay roughage blend/grass, sans molasses grain, and minor element salt will guarantee that your dwarf gets every one of the supplements they need.

On the off chance that you need to raise your Pygmy goat, the ideal opportunity to stand by is year and a half after they're conceived.

CHAPTER 5

THE PYGMY GOAT PRIZING & PROFIT, MILK AS WELL AS FOR MEAT

Pygmy Goats Price

Pygmy goats cost differ broadly relying upon whether you are content with an unregistered creature to keep as a pet ($40-$50), or need a pedigreed Pygmy to begin rearing of your own available to be purchased and benefit in the range ($150 - $300).

Pygmy Goat Breeders

Since Pygmies are the two pets and animals, there are assortments of raisers who represent considerable authority in various purposes.

Numerous mainstream Pygmy reproducers can just be found on social media, and there are brilliant assets accessible through the National Pygmy Goat Association.

Be careful about individuals offering pet goats through open release sheets. Ensure you visit the goat on location prior to bringing it home, checking that the goat is solid and parasite free, and that its everyday environments are spotless and sound.

Getting back a wiped out goat not exclusively can prompt broad costly veterinary consideration, and possibly the deficiency of the creature, however can place your different creatures in wellbeing danger too. It's ideal to consistently purchase from a raiser with a decent standing, and review the goat completely before you consent to get it.

African Pygmy Goat

The Pygmy goat is likewise alluded to as the African dwarf and the small goat. They're a smaller than normal type of goat that can undoubtedly adjust to their current circumstance, notwithstanding various environments.

What are Pygmy goats utilized for?

Pygmy goats are solid, little creatures that have the most amiable of characters. Their little height and amicableness make them staggering show creatures. They weigh as much as 65 pounds and however they're little and charming, Pygmy goats can stand their ground in milk creation and rearing.

Pygmy goats as pets

Pygmy goats are known to be charming, agreeable, and arrive in a wide range of shadings. In case you're hoping to house any as pets, there are a couple of things you should think about them, as they do require an alternate degree of care than your normal family creature.

Every Pygmy is extraordinary, and their perspectives are diverse too. Despite the fact that most are cordial, some might be somewhat distant from the outset. Pygmy goats are extremely lively.

As a pet, Pygmies require new, clean water and a lot of nutritious food varieties.

A little, solid, ventilated construction is a decent spot to keep your pygmy/dwarf goat.

Pygmy goats for meat

In case you're setting up your goat ranch to be a wellspring of meat, you need to realize that there are show goats, and afterward there are meat goats. They're raised in an unexpected way, so when you're choosing your variety, ensure you understand what kind of goat you're getting.

Despite the fact that they're little in size, dwarf goat meat sells since it's so minimal. Additionally, they mate unavailable and breed each 9 to a year. This implies that this specific variety creates seriously posterity for more meat.

Pygmy goats for milk

At the pinnacle of their lactation, Pygmy goats can deliver up to ⅔ of a gallon of milk each day. Their milk is sweet and tasty. Pygmy goats' milk is best kept up when it's kept in chilly stockpiling.

Pygmy goat milk is wealthy in calcium, potassium, and lower in sodium than different varieties.

CHAPTER 6

THE PYGMY GOATS DISEASES OR AILMENTS PLUS OTHER FACTS

Regular Diseases of Pygmy Goats/ Goats

Goats harbour a few types of coccidia yet not all show clinical coccidiosis. Grown-up pygmy goats or goats shed coccidia in excrement, defile the climate, and contaminate the infant. As disease pressure develops in the pens, dreariness in kids conceived later increments. Signs incorporate the runs or pale defecation, loss of condition, general feebleness, and inability to develop. In peracute cases, children may kick the bucket without clinical signs. Turning every one of the children through a couple of pens is risky. To help forestall coccidiosis in misleadingly raised dairy goats, the children ought to be placed in little, age-coordinated with bunches in outside, versatile pens that are moved to clean ground occasionally. Annihilation isn't attainable, yet disease can be controlled through acceptable administration rehearses. Coccidiostats added to the water or feed are extras to an administration control program and not substitutes. Constant coccidiosis is one of the fundamental driver of helpless development in kids and is answerable for the uneconomical act of postponing rearing for a year until the goat has arrived at sufficient size (70 lb [32 kg] for dairy breeds). In Angora goats kept widely, the issue is seen at weaning, when the children are kept in more modest parcels and took care of supplement on the ground.

In fed and free-running goats, helminthiasis can expect incredible clinical importance. GI nematodiasis, liver accident pervasion, and lungworm contaminations all might be seen. Age-related protection from parasitism in goats is frail comparative with that in different ruminants. Albeit generally normal in yearlings during their first season on field, clinical parasitism might be found in grown-ups also. Helpless development, weight reduction, the runs, a messy hair coat, indications of weakness, and intermandibular edema (bottle jaw) might be seen with GI parasitism or liver accident infection. Haemonchus contortus contamination has arisen as a significant imperative in the extending meat goat industry in the southeastern USA. Steady hacking in pre-fall and pre-winter is the standard show of lungworms; auxiliary bacterial pneumonia with fever is a typical sequela. Parasitism is slippery on interest ranches, where the issue may not exist for quite a while and afterward unexpectedly detonates as goat numbers proceed to increment and offices become overloaded. Tapeworm proglottids are regularly noted in goat excrement by proprietors. Despite the fact that tapeworms are not for the most part viewed as of clinical significance, their revelation can be utilized to survey the subject of helminthiasis with proprietors and foster a general parasite control program (see **Gastrointestinal Parasites of Sheep and Pygmy Goats or Goats).**

Clostridium perfringens type D can be lethal, and it isn't constantly connected with the exemplary change in quality as well as volume of feed. In issue crowds, inoculation each 4–6 mo might be fundamental, since goats may not keep up defensive insusceptibility as long as sheep or dairy cattle when given similar business antibodies. Inoculation forestalls the intense demise condition, however sometimes even immunized goats may foster intense enteritis. Influenced goats foster serious looseness of the bowels and significant wretchedness; milk yield drops unexpectedly. Demise may happen in 24 hr. Treatment includes organization of counteragent, analgesics, liquid treatment, amendment of acidosis, and anti-infection agents.

Inoculation for infectious ecthyma (sore mouth, see Contagious Ecthyma) isn't demonstrated except if the illness exists in the vicinity. The principle issues with tainted children are trouble in nursing, spreading sores to the does' udders or the collaborators' hands, and participation at goat shows being denied. Live infection antibody is utilized by scarifying the skin (eg, inside the thighs or under the tail) and painting on the immunization. Both normal injuries and those subsequent from inoculation may keep going up to 4 wk, yet after the scabs have dropped off, the goats can go to shows.

Constant squandering is seen regularly; it's anything but a solitary infection yet a condition. By and large, if a goat is all around took care of, kept in a tranquil climate, and has great teeth and a low parasite load, it ought to flourish and create. In the event that it doesn't, and starts "squandering," it ought to be separated right away. The significant reasons for ongoing squandering incorporate helpless nourishment, parasitism, dental issues, paratuberculosis, interior instinctive abscesses because of Corynebacterium pseudotuberculosis (ovis) or Trueperella pyogenes, locomotor issues (especially joint inflammation because of retrovirus contamination [CAE virus]), and persistent secret diseases like metritis, peritonitis, or pneumonia. Tumors are every so often analyzed in more seasoned goats. These sicknesses are once in a while treatable, and many are infectious; this is the reason for the exacting separating strategy, which is indispensable to the general efficiency of a group.

Paratuberculosis in goats contrasts from that in dairy cattle; net posthumous injuries are less articulated and abundant, the runs happens less normally in goats until just before death. Subsequently, numerous cases may go undiscovered until necropsy. The ileocecal hub is the most remunerating tissue for bacteriologic culture and histopathology. Symptomatic testing for caprine paratuberculosis incorporates agar gel immunodiffusion, pooled fluid fecal culture, direct fecal PCR, etc. The control program for paratuberculosis in goats is like that in dairy cattle.

Caprine joint inflammation and infection has arisen as a significant irresistible specialist of seriously raised dairy goats, however all types of goats are defenceless to this retrovirus. CAE disease in goats can show from numerous points of view: subclinical, determined contamination; a reformist paresis of youthful goats 2–12 months old; agalactia with a firm, non-inflamed udder at parturition in reproduced females; or a ligament condition with torment and swollen joints in grown-ups. A constant, reformist interstitial pneumonia or a squandering condition may likewise be found in grown-ups. CAE disease has been thought about basically to be spread from dam to posterity through infection loaded colostrum and milk, and control programs have been pointed toward isolating the infants from the grown-up populace and taking care of warmth treated colostrum and sanitized milk. Contamination may continue in crowds in which this is rehearsed because of level transmission between grown-ups. Normal testing and thorough separating of every single seropositive goat, or exacting isolation of seropositive and seronegative goats, should be polished if sickness annihilation is the objective.

Routine Vaccination Programs

Most goat crowds regularly immunize for lockjaw and for enterotoxemia (Clostridium perfringens composed C and D). Choices to consolidate extra immunizations for abortifacients, infectious ecthyma, abscesses, gram-negative microorganisms or respiratory illness into the crowd wellbeing plan will be founded on the individual requirements of the group and the conceivable danger of every sickness in the crowd. Exact records of illness and fetus removal and research facility analyze where required are basic in suggesting immunizations for each crowd.

Overseeing Reproduction in the Pygmy Goat Herd

In the Pygmy goat group, conceptive execution will at last decide the quantity of rearing females, crowd sires or others delivered every year. Getting ready for group size regulation (intentionally not reproducing a few creatures) can help enhance other crowd wellbeing assets. Exact reproducing records, arranged rearing and joking procedures and avoidance of fetus removal are critical to augmenting the wellbeing of the crowd. Utilizing transabdominal ultrasonography to affirm reproducing (due) dates and decide litter size can assist proprietors with arranging joking administration, including the potential for enlistment of parturition for high danger pregnancies like those at higher danger of requiring cesarean segments. Escalated checking and the executives of joking can decrease the quantity of stillbirths and dam mortality by advancing early mediation in instances of dystocia. Analysis and control of infectious fetus removal is a significant piece of conceptive wellbeing the board.

Checking for Genetic Defects as Well as Diseases

Reproducers ought to be ready for deserts that are clear at the hour of birth like malocclusion, appendage disfigurements or cryptorchidism. Other innate conditions or illnesses may not be perceived until after the neonatal period. For instance, the acquired condition Pygmy goat myelofibrosis (basic passive legacy) makes kids be sickly and neglect to flourish, however signs are by and large perceived when the children are a long time to months old. Documentation of family and precise rearing records are basic to perceiving possibly acquired conditions which the basic etiology may some way or another go unseen.

Parasite Management And Control

Coccidiosis is a significant reason for diminished development rates and clinical illness in a wide range of goat crowds. Giving one of the coccidiostats (decoquinate, lasalocid, rumensin, amprolium) to developing children to forestall clinical infection, brief location and treatment of clinical sickness (for instance, with sulfadimethoxine) and counteraction of fecal tainting of feeds through feed bunk the board are basic components to control of coccidiosis in goat crowds. The overall significance of inside parasites like Haemonchus, other intestinal parasites, lungworms, liver accidents or outside parasites will rely extraordinarily upon the environment, sort of activity (dry part, field, peruse), taking care of/field the board and earlier history of parasite control. Anthelmintic opposition has prompted utilization of the FAMACHA strategy for particular Haemonchus treatment. Notwithstanding approach, continuous observation through faecal egg checks or necropsy ought to be utilized to devise the most reasonable way to deal with parasite the board.

More on Pygmy Goats Diseases

Johne's Disease

Pygmy goats' crowds may have undetected Johne's infection because of little group size and long brooding period. Joking isolation and cleanliness can diminish hazard of openness to Mycobacterium avium subspp paratuberculosis (MAP) in the maternity climate. Johne's illness hazard evaluation in the Pygmy groups ought to incorporate steers, sheep different goats and other Johne's-vulnerable species as a feature of a general ranch plan. Accessibility of moderate testing by serology and additionally faecal culture for MAP contamination changes from state-to-state. Explicit testing procedures are less distinct for goats than for dairy cattle. Also, inoculation techniques might be conceivable in tainted crowds under the participation of administrative veterinarians.

Scrapie

Despite the fact that scrapie isn't common in Pygmy goats, Pygmy goats are dependent upon the National Scrapie Eradication Program (NSEP) rules, and reconnaissance for and avoidance of presentation of scrapie into Pygmy goat groups is basic. Crowd substitution sources ought to give official ID and trace back data, and purchasers should investigate for potential danger related with blending of Pygmy goats with lambing ewes or joking does. The crowd wellbeing plan ought to incorporate necropsy of all creatures with ongoing squandering and additionally reformist neurologic signs. Dwarf goats should conform to NSEP distinguishing proof guidelines. Enlisted goats joined by their enrolment endorsement and moved to the current proprietor may use enlistment electronic ID or tattoos. Unregistered creatures and all creatures travelling through places of focus (public market) require scrapie program ear labels.

Continuous Disease Surveillance

In more modest Pygmy goat groups similarly likewise with all goat crowds, fruitful control for persistent infections depends on proceeded with illness reconnaissance. It might take more time to decide sickness designs in the little crowd and without butcher observing as a device; however similar group wellbeing standards apply. The executives choices in regards to infectious prevention gathering, treatment, multiplication and separating ought to be. In view of precise long lasting records on every creature. Exceptional individual creature recognizable proof (tattoos, electronic ID, and so forth) is expected to before perpetual precise records can be kept up to screen irresistible illness status. Dam illness status is required as a component of the lasting doe record. Arranged routine necropsy of geriatric creatures eliminated from the group and well as passing and fetus removals will permit observing for all significant benefactors of infection in the crowd, not simply essential driver of death. Extra testing for tissue copper and selenium, parasites and different things of interest can help distinguish simultaneous infection issues which may perplex the endeavours of a particular infectious prevention program. Johne's sickness, scrapie, CLA, CAEV, and Mycoplasma would all be able to be observed by necropsy despite the fact that the reason for death might be disconnected to these illnesses. Serologic testing for CLA or CAEV might be essential for a continuous control program for the crowd or used to screen new group presentations. Continuous serologic reconnaissance for CAEV will permit powerful isolation of contaminated creatures to diminish grown-up transmission of infection. Milk societies for Staphylococcus aureus, Mycoplasma spp, and other infectious microbes take into account continuous decrease or disposal procedures.

CHAPTER 7

REARING CHICKENS WITH YOUR AMAZING PYGMY GOATS

Regardless of whether you're thinking about adding goats to chickens (or chickens to goats), it's critical to know whether it's feasible to have both together. Also, it's much more imperative to realize how to keep them together. So we should discuss some genuine tips on keeping chickens and goats together.

Chickens and goats can live respectively with appropriate arrangement and plans to incorporate them securely. Issues to address incorporate lodging, field sharing versus turning, feed, waste, and general wellbeing, all things considered.

Would chickens be able to Live Successfully with Goats?

Yes. Chickens and goats can be kept together without any problem. It's done around the world – and is even suggested by different government offices – as long as it's done securely.

Give Separate Living Spaces to Goats and Chickens

Goats and chickens will require separate living spaces for two primary reasons.

1.   Chickens like to perch on a roost while they rest.

2.   Chickens crap on everything.

Giving your goats and chickens a different living space will likewise forestall different issues, similar to inadvertent trampling, butting, and pecking.

Notwithstanding, this doesn't mean they need separate structures. Goats and chickens can share a stable – they'll simply require separate zones inside that outbuilding.

You can do this by utilizing a type of chicken wire or wire fencing to cordon off the chicken's territory. At that point, contingent upon the kind of fencing utilized, the chickens can either get through the fence or pass through a devoted entryway territory to get to their different living quarters.

What goats need in their quarters

Inside your goat's indoor territory, they'll need a couple of essential things. These include:

•	An territory to lay down with clean sheet material. Goats will most likely crap in it any time you set down crisp sheet material, however.

•	Separate joking slows down for guarding infant and developing children from your group.

•	An discretionary, separate draining slow down for in the event that you need to drain your goats inside. That way, goats will not utilize it as a washroom – and your draining territory will remain more clean.

- An indoor feed and water station.

- Reinforced or tough dividers and parts for when the goats incline toward them.

- Minimal (in a perfect world zero) spots to roost over the goats' regions.

You might need to have a type of an implicit feed rack, as well. Simply ensure it doesn't have something on top of it that will draw in chickens – or urge your goats to climb it.

Since while goats love to eat new feed, they will not eat dirtied feed. Also, anything that has been crapped on it (by fowl or another goat) certainly qualifies as dirty.

What your chickens will require around there

Inside the chicken territory, you'll need a couple of things for them. They include:

- Roosting bars or roosts.
- Nesting boxes for laying eggs.
- Feed and on-request supplements.
- Water.

We'll discuss why you need their food and water in their indoor territory later on in this article – in the part about keeping goat and chicken feed independent.

Training Chickens to Stay as well as Lay in their Coop's Nesting Containers

There's a great reality about chickens: they all prefer to utilize the equivalent settling box. It doesn't appear to issue the number of chickens you have – they all need to utilize the well known laying area.

In any case, we can utilize this for our potential benefit with the goal that chickens aren't laying eggs in the goats' feed.

At the point when you move your chickens to another area, train them to utilize their coop around evening time. What's more, train them to utilize gave settling boxes.

Here's the means by which we did it, in view of proposals found in my exploration.

1.   When you move chickens to another space, start by saving them inside the coop for a couple of days.

2.   If your chickens are still pullets, keep the settling boxes closed off – so they don't utilize them yet.

3.   After a couple of days, let your chickens/pullets out into the run. Each evening, ensure they're back inside and lock it up. Along these lines, they'll figure out how to head inside and be shielded from hunters.

4.   After a couple of days or weeks, you would then be able to allow your chickens to approach their field, as well.

5.   Your chickens will take care of themselves every evening.

At the point when we do add goats and a stable, we'll need to re-do these means when we acquaint our chickens with their new, still-hypothetical home. All things considered, we'll need to add a 6th and seventh step when that occurs.

- Once your chickens are prepared to figure out how to lay, open up the settling boxes or give a territory to home and lay. Consider placing an earthenware egg in a settling box or two to show the chickens where to lay.

- For the principal bit, ensure they are back inside by dull and be keeping watch for any chickens meandering into the goats' living quarters. Shoo them out.

It's a decent piece of work forthright, without a doubt. Yet, by doing this from the start, you'll have the option to save yourself a great deal of additional work over the long haul. Furthermore, as we add chickens to our group, we'll have the more established chicken's assistance in preparing the new options.

As far as we might be concerned, the forthright work was definitely justified. Our chickens love to meander their smaller than normal field space, yet they additionally will return to their run and coop for feed, water, supplements, and to lay eggs in the given settling boxes.

Think about Pasture Options Carefully

With regards to keeping goats and chickens together, you need to consider your field choices cautiously. There two or three choices for field spaces.

- You can keep goats and chickens in a similar field.

- You can keep chickens and goats in isolated fields.

- You can turn pastures, keeping chickens and goats together.

- You can turn pastures, keeping goats and chickens discrete.

Your accessible field space will affect how you decide to pasture your creatures – and whether you keep the goats separate from the chickens or not.

Since we've just got 0.1 sections of land of field space, we're inclining towards keeping our chickens and goats in the equivalent, solitary field. We're unquestionably still in the arranging and working it out stage, however.

Another significant factor in field space is fencing. What amount fencing would you say you will introduce to have separate field space? We like the possibility of less establishment of wall, so a solitary, shared field likewise wins around there! In any event, it accomplishes for us. You'll need to choose how you need your field spaces separated.

Cross-Species Behavioural as well as Injury Risks

On the off chance that you keep any creatures together, there is an inborn danger for interspecies infection, injury, and passing. It would sure be decent if the entirety of the creatures would get along constantly – yet it doesn't occur. Mishaps occur. We will initially discuss the wounds and mishaps.

For chickens and goats, my exploration demonstrates that keeping them together can end in a few sorts of wounds.

Goats can make the accompanying kinds of wounds one another or your poultry.

- Stomping or stomping on wounds.
- Blunt power injury brought about by butting.
- Crushing wounds from falling, hopping, or sitting on different creatures.

Chickens can cause different sorts of wounds. They may incorporate any of the accompanying.

- Pecking wounds, particularly whenever compromised or they see blood (chickens don't endure shortcoming).

- Slashing wounds from chicken's prods.
- Scratching wounds from any chicken's feet – they're small scale hooks, all things considered!

In case you're saving chickens for eggs, recall that either species (chickens or goats) may annihilate eggs – either coincidentally or intentionally. It'll rely upon where the egg was laid or on the off chance that they've fostered a preference for eggs.

Alright, so in my examination, I've never known about an egg-eating goat. On the off chance that something is eating your eggs, it's presumably either a chicken (search for pecking harm), a pet (particularly a canine who loves eggs), or a hunter – like a rat inhabitant examining the neighbourhood food.

Keep Feed and Supplements Separated

How about we start with the self-evident: goat feed is figured for goats. Chicken feed is figured for chickens. Each sort of feed will not function admirably for the other creature. Thus, keep goats out of the chicken feed and chickens out of the goat feed.

In my exploration, the most serious issue with goats getting into chicken feed is that it's a major change from their standard feed. Furthermore, any unexpected change in a goat's eating routine can cause the runs, bulge, and even passing.

Thus, we should feel free to keep the goats out of the chicken feed – and the chickens out of the goat feed. However, – how would we do that?

Instructions to keep backs down of the goat feed

In light of my exploration, goat feed, by and large, isn't needed. Goats will do alright with scrounging and eating-quality feed. I have perused that it's a smart thought to give pregnant or draining does a modest bunch of grain every morning.

On the off chance that they're pregnant, give them a modest bunch of grain or so every morning when you go keep an eye on them. For draining does, give them a little container (with a small bunch or so of grain) in it to eat while they're being drained. That way, no different creatures are getting into your (costly) grain stash.

At that point, simply keep your huge reserve of grain in an aluminium garbage bin – that way, you will not draw in any rodents. Mice and rodents could eat through a plastic tub – yet aluminium is rat evidence.

On the off chance that you do need to utilize goat feed, don't surrender – it's as yet conceivable to keep the chickens out of it. Simply limit when the goat feed is out – to when you're out there and present. Goats needn't bother with feed that is out constantly, particularly on the off chance that they do have some field and roughage, as well. So you could absolutely deal with feed as you do a grain supplement.

In the event that the chickens are dreadfully energetic about the goats' feed, ensure you feed the goats before you let the chickens out of their coop or run. That ought to likewise be a tremendous tip to keeping the chickens out! The most effective method to keep goats out of chicken feed.

The most ideal approach to do that is to have two separate care taking areas.

1.   Inside the coop or chicken space of an outbuilding, hang a feeder brimming with the proper feed for your chickens. Chickens can eat feed on request.

2.   Outside of the coop, let chickens scavenge and scratch for whatever they can discover and need to eat. Try not to keep any feed outside of the coop.

At that point, your chickens will require a chicken-sized access to their committed region. We utilize a programmed entryway as the passage. That way, it's little enough for a solitary chicken at a time – and we additionally don't need to go open or close it consistently to give the chickens day by day admittance to the field.

Our chickens have a balancing feeder in their indoor coop and run territory. That way, they can eat anything they desire. We likewise keep their squashed clam shell in their coop and run territory. We likewise keep a 5-gallon container (with watering areolas) in there so they can generally get water.

Yet, on the off chance that our chickens need to scrounge for bugs and whatever else they need? Simple – they simply go out their programmed chicken entryway into their field. On the off chance that they at any point need a beverage of clean water or some chicken feed, they simply head once more into their coop and run.

That way, chicken feed is free from any and all harm – and away from different creatures that shouldn't eat it in any case.

Chickens and goats are additionally stunning on the grounds that they can assist you with limiting waste – particularly in case you're into treating the soil. Be that as it may, don't stress – we'll talk over fertilizing the soil later on in the guide.

All things considered, goats can assist you with diminishing and cycle bunches of weeds that different creatures will not touch. Also, that is absolutely helpful for weed control – particularly in light of the fact that they can eat a ton of plants that are harmful to different creatures (like toxic substance ivy).

Chickens can likewise assist you with lessening and reuse a ton of things – much extra eggs and disposed of feed that the goats presently will not touch.

My chickens love assisting me with preparing utilized kitchen scraps – regardless of whether they're offered straightforwardly to them or they uncover it from my fertilizer heap on the off chance that I neglect to close the nursery entryway.

I've likewise known about certain homesteaders who assemble the grain their goats didn't eat – and they add that to any additional goat milk. At that point, they'll dump the additional grain into the milk and let it sit for the time being. Obviously, it will make a delicate cheddar that their chickens love to eat. It is anything but a strategy I've at any point attempted, however it's very a cool stunt and approach to not waste milk.

Regardless, don't feel awful about reusing anything you can – as long as you do it securely. It's an incredible method to limit your general impression and live more dependably as a patio homesteader.

Oversee Manure – in the event that you can!

In the event that you will keep the two chickens and goats, you will have fertilizer all over the place. The two goats and chickens drop heaps of manure any place they are and at whatever point they must go.

The issue with fertilizer all over is the point at which it's excessively near food and water sources. At that point, any germs or bugs in the crap can turn into an immense tainting issue – particularly for different creatures!

So you'll need to get imaginative with how you oversee compost – and how you feed and water the two arrangements of creatures.

For overseeing compost, here are a couple of tips and thoughts that may work, in view of my experience and examination.

- Use effectively scooped filler (straw, pine pellets, or pine shavings) for bedding. That way, tidy up can be simpler – and all that waste can be added to your fertilizer heap. We'll discuss manure in one moment.

- Use a draping chicken feeder with a cover – to keep chickens from crapping in their own feed.

- Use a feed rack that is less appealing to chickens. Eliminate anything over the feed that would pull in the chickens to need to roost over the goats' food – and crap on it.

- Keep water sources as spotless as could really be expected. Think about utilizing a top on the water – and afterward use watering areolas if your creatures can utilize them. You can peruse my article about keeping chickens' water clean and green growth free here or look at this one on the most proficient method to keep water clean for chicks (with pictures).

In view of my exploration, goats might be prepared to utilize. Utilizing that water areola feeder would allow you to utilize a huge, lidded water source like a 55-gallon pail. That way, it would be a ton simpler to keep chicken excrement out of watering sources. It would likewise scale back water misfortune from vanishing and creatures pushing it over, as well.

These tips will assist you with overseeing compost – yet it will not forestall it totally.

Bantam goats and chickens are simply so darn charming.

Figure out how to Be OK with Goat and Chicken Dung

Indeed, even with the entirety of the most astonishing excrement overseeing tips, there's as yet going to be a ton of crap. So you must figure out how to approve of a ton of crap.

One tip that is assisted me with learning be better with creature excrement (or compost – anyway you need to call it) is by keeping my creatures in a contained space of my yard.

That way, I've just had the opportunity to tidy up the assigned zones – I actually have a terrace that is for our family. All things being equal, I do need to tidy up canine crap from that space... there's generally such a lot of crap!

The subsequent tip is to figure out how to compost.

Figure out how to Compost Chicken Plus Goat Manure

At the point when you keep chickens and goats, you will have a terrible parcel of compost accumulating. In contrast to my canine's crap, be that as it may, this fertilizer can be treated with the soil – and it's extraordinary for your patio property garden!

Treating the soil doesn't need to be extravagant – or require any kind of extravagant turning composter. The turning composters do accelerate the cycle, yet they seriously limit amounts – except if you pay more for the greater, multi-chambered adaptations. And still, at the end of the day, not every one of them get extraordinary audits.

All things considered, we decided on straightforward effectiveness.

Regardless, it's two one next to the other squares of pressing factor treated wood, chicken wire, screws, and staples. Notwithstanding, each side is bounty large for an entire period of compost, bedding, and nursery scraps.

Also, due to how we layer the compost, scraps, bedding, and outbuilding lime, we don't need to do anything with it – and it doesn't smell at all or draw in any bugs.

It's the simplest method to compost. Also, in the spring? I have a decent measured heap of characteristic, fertilizer upgraded manure to add to my nursery.

Truth be told, the solitary main problem we've encountered with fertilizing the soil is that the chickens love to get into it when I neglect to close the nursery door. At that point, they're spreading the fertilizer for me – and eating who knows what!

In any case, on the off chance that you put your manure in a different segment of your yard, that should eliminate the chickens getting into it. Simply recall to close the entryway!

Try not to expect goats or chickens to protect each other – however they may astonish you!

The following tip is that goats and chickens may not effectively secure one another. So in case you're thinking about getting goats to ensure your chickens, you'd likely improve a watchman canine, a llama, or even an alpaca.

Nonetheless, there are unquestionably stories where goats and chickens do ensure and really focus on one another.

• Active security: stories where goats or chickens effectively protect each other are uncommon – they're the special case instead of the standard.

• Passive security: keeping these creatures together may offer some latent assurance, as each may help caution different types of threat or fill in as a characteristic obstacle to certain hunters.

Some bigger types of goats might be better dynamic safeguards – particularly on the off chance that you get maimed guys that actually have horns. Nonetheless, at that point you have a goat with horns – and that may turn into a security issue for your group or your family.

So you truly need to gauge the upsides and downsides in any case.

For our situation, we're inclining towards Nigerian bantam goats – so they won't be an excess of greater than our chickens. All things considered, we aren't anticipating that they should be stunning or dynamic watchmen for our chickens. What's more, we likewise don't expect that our chickens will do a lot to effectively ensure the goats.

Notwithstanding, we'll coordinate them as a solitary, blended species crowd. What's more, thusly, we're trusting they'll caution each other of risk. Furthermore, just by having the goats around, that should give our group a little additional proportion of insurance from winged hunters.

Learn Basic Animal Care and First Aid

The real tip to keeping chickens and goats together is to gain proficiency with some essential medical aid and creature care. You'll likewise have to know a few fundamentals of chicken and goat brain science.

- Chickens, for instance, don't give early indications of ailment or shortcoming. Chances are that the main indications of sickness you see will be later signs – and it's difficult to do much by then.

- Chickens likewise don't endure shortcoming – or wounds – in their herd since it puts the entire rush in danger of being hunter lure. In this way, in the event that you do have a harmed or draining chicken, different chickens will really assault them.

- Goats will not assault one another, yet they will play unpleasant now and again. In any case, if a goat inadvertently harms another creature (goat or chicken), you'll need to watch out for them – particularly if there's any draining included. You may even have to isolate them from the remainder of your group and crowd to really focus on them while they mend.

To do this, you'll need to know some fundamental emergency treatment – creature style. Fortunately, there are heaps of extraordinary YouTube recordings that show you fundamental creature medical aid. Also, on the off chance that you need to follow us on YouTube, we'd love it! Simply look for our Backyard Homestead HQ channel – and you'll see us.

Being a (human) nurture with trauma centre insight, this is the place where I feel a slight benefit – regardless of whether I do in any case watch veterinarian channels to ensure I keep up on the most proficient method to really focus on my creatures.

Since once you realize how to really focus on creatures after all other options have been exhausted, you will feel a dreadful parcel safer in all the other things. And afterward you'll truly have the option to partake in having your goats and chickens together in your patio property!

More on Keeping Goats with Chickens; More Explanations

There are in excess of a couple of homesteaders keeping goats with chickens in similar pens or field territories just as having a similar lodging. Some never have any issues or issues however blending chickens and goats can make issues that one might need to keep away from. One genuine, potential issue is a minuscule parasite, known as Cryptosporidium. A few sorts of this parasite are explicit, which means they are not effectively moved between various creatures. Tragically, there are different types of Cryptosporidium that are not host-explicit, and can undoubtedly move between various types of creatures including goats, chickens, sheep, cows or even people. They are frequently spread through a faecal-oral transmission course.

Sullied drinking water is the most widely recognized strategy for transmission. In any case, Cryptosporidium can be moved through the dirty sheet material, tainted feed, or some other possible medium in creature lodging. The life forms are omnipresent, which means

They are all over the place. They can be difficult to kill and are impervious to chlorine-based cleaning specialists.

The parasites can cause intestinal irritation or enteritis in child goats just as different ruminants. Serious loose bowels, which can be lethal, and intestinal draining happen. In certain spaces of the world, including India, extreme misfortunes happen each year in the goat business on account of Cryptosporidium.

Cryptosporidium contaminations can likewise be wrecking to chickens and other fowl. They can taint the bursa of the lungs, windpipe, sinuses or intestinal parcel. Diseases can get deadly. Since chickens and other fowl are infamous for leaving defecation wherever they go, including drinking water and feed troughs, it is a smart thought to have separate lodging courses of action for your goats (or sheep) and chickens.

Other major issues can happen when keeping goats with chickens as a result of significant degrees of Salmonella enterica and Campylobacter microorganisms, which are both present in poultry defecation. Doe or other ruminant udders can be sullied with one or the other microbes and afterward move them to the nursing posterity. Low degrees of either microscopic organism can be lethal to youthful ruminants. Child goats are additionally famously inquisitive and can ingest poultry droppings. Two types of Campylobacter microscopic organisms, the two of which are zoonotic in nature, which means they are not host-explicit, are C. jejuni and C. coli. Momentum research discoveries have pinpointed these two microscopic organisms cause issues.

Separate Food

The greatest issue you'll confront when your goats and chickens live respectively is keeping them out of one another's food.

Goats love chicken feed, however it's basic you keep them clear of it. On the off chance that your goats get into chicken feed, they may wind up experiencing the runs and swell — and if it's extreme enough, it very well may be lethal.

Chickens aren't probably going to experience the ill effects of eating goat feed. Nonetheless, they aren't specific about where they leave their droppings — and in the event that they end up being roosted on the edge of the goat trough, it's responsible to land in the goats' roughage. Goats will not eat dirtied feed, which means you'll need to toss it out and give them a new group. Squandered roughage implies squandered cash.

You can cure this issue various ways. Start by keeping chicken feed in a draping feeder inside their coop. Ensure the coop has openings sufficiently enormous for your chickens to get in and out, yet little enough that goats can't enter. Feed any grain to your goats before you discharge the chickens toward the beginning of the day and after you lock them up around evening time. Store your goats' feed in a trough with a top so the chickens can't get in it to lay or perch.

Separate Housing

It's totally fine to let chickens and goats free roaming together, however they do require their very own position when not ended up. You'll have to give the chickens a spot to live liberated from the goats where they can be warm and shielded from hunters. The goats require a haven liberated from the chickens, as perching birds will leave droppings on whatever is beneath and scratch up dirtied bedding.

Make Sure You Lock Coop Doors- Inquisitive goats would climb right in as well as eat chicken feed

The actual yard shouldn't be anything extraordinary — simply ensure it's fenced well. Goat boards with four-inch openings should function admirably on the off chance that you have bigger varieties. On the off chance that you have dwarves or dwarfs, go for boards with more modest openings (two x four inch) to hold your children back from loosening up. While the goat boards are pleasant, electric wire or mesh might be bound to keep your creatures in and hunters out in a similar time. On the off chance that you do choose to go the electric highway, a 5000-volt charger will work for both the goats and the chickens.

Injury

The most well-known injury you'll observe when you keep your Pygmy goats as well as chickens together is a crushed chicken foot. Goats aren't especially aware of where they step, and if a chicken isn't adequately fast, such things will undoubtedly occur. Goats may get a sharp peck on the gag; however that is likely the most difficulty they'll get from their chicken companions.

Infection

Infections are something else completely. Coccidiosis is a typical worry among goat and chicken proprietors. Nonetheless, coccidia is explicit, which means it can't be spread from chickens to goats and the other way around. Cryptosporidiosis, brought about by the protozoan cryptosporidium, is an intestinal parasite that influences the birds and warm blooded animals. Cryptosporidiosis isn't unprecedented in bound youthful chickens and can be deadly to kids.

Salmonella microorganisms live in the digestion tracts of chickens and since chickens leave droppings anyplace, it can without much of a stretch be spread. In the event that a doe rests in ruined sheet material, her udder can get polluted. A child that consequently nurture from said udder can get a deadly portion of salmonella.

Keep your goat shed, chicken coop, and yard as perfect as could really be expected. In the event that any of your creatures start giving indications of ailment, isolate them and call a vet right away. The sooner they are dealt with, the almost certain they are to endure.

Why Keep Them Together At All?

With all the additional work included, you may ask why you ought to try and try keeping chickens and goats together by any means. Chickens are useful for eliminating food squander from goats — they get grain the goats drop. Chickens likewise eat bugs and parasites that make their homes around the goats' pen. The two creatures give the other friendship — now and again in any event, shaping solid interspecies bonds.

CHAPTER 8

CONCLUSION

Having gone through the nitty-gritty of pygmy goats; I am sure you will stick to the guidelines of caring/ nurturing your amazing pygmy goats as well as rearing chickens with them.

Remember, there no shot-cuts to caring for your new pet (Pygmy Goats).

All the best to you!

THE END.

www.ingramcontent.com/pod-product-compliance
Ingram Content Group UK Ltd.
Pitfield, Milton Keynes, MK11 3LW, UK
UKHW021320010625
6177UKWH00028B/976